Math Counts

NUMBERS

Children's Press®
An Imprint of Scholastic Inc.

About This Series

In keeping with the major goals of the National Council of Teachers of Mathematics, children will become mathematical problem solvers, learn to communicate mathematically, and learn to reason mathematically by using the series Math Counts.

Pattern, Shape, and *Size* may be investigated first—in any sequence.

Sorting, Counting, and *Numbers* may be used next, followed by *Time, Length, Weight,* and *Capacity.*

—Ramona G. Choos, Professor of Mathematics,
Senior Adviser to the Dean of Continuing Education, Chicago State University;
Sponsor for Chicago Elementary Teachers' Mathematics Club

Author's Note

Mathematics is a part of a child's world. It is not only interpreting numbers or mastering tricks of addition or multiplication. Mathematics is about ideas. These ideas have been developed to explain particular qualities such as size, weight, and height, as well as relationships and comparisons. Yet all too often the important part that an understanding of mathematics will play in a child's development is forgotten or ignored.

Most adults can solve simple mathematical tasks without the need for counters, beads, or fingers. Young children find such abstractions almost impossible to master. They need to see, talk, touch, and experiment.

The photographs and text in these books have been chosen to encourage talk about topics that are essentially mathematical. By talking, the young reader can explore some of the central concepts that support mathematics. It is on an understanding of these concepts that a student's future mastery of mathematics will be built.

—Henry Pluckrose

Math Counts

NUMBERS

By Henry Pluckrose

Mathematics Consultant: Ramona G. Choos, Professor of Mathematics

Children's Press®
An Imprint of Scholastic Inc.

There are numbers all around us.
There are numbers on houses

and on cars.

You can find numbers on telephones

and on money.

Numbers help us in many ways.
How do these road signs help drivers?

WEST

EAST

INTERSTATE
NEW MEXICO
10

INTERSTATE
NEW MEXICO
10

↑ LORDSBURG

DEMING →

8

These buses have route numbers.
How does this help passengers?

Numbers give information. The numbers on these cartons tell us how much each one holds.

These shoes have a number printed on the back.
What do the numbers tell you? What is your shoe size?

Months are counted in days. Each day has a number. What is today's date?

8 AUGUST

SUN	MON	TUE	WED	THU	FRI	SAT
	1	2	3	4	5	6
7	8	9	10	11	12	13
14	15	16	17	18	19	20
21	22	23	24	25	26	27
28	29	30	31			

7 JULY

SUN	MON	TUE	WED	THU	FRI	SAT
					1	2
3	4	5	6	7	8	9
10	11	12	13	14	15	16
17	18	19	20	21	22	23
24 31	25	26	27	28	29	30

9 SEPTEMBER

SUN	MON	TUE	WED	THU	FRI	SAT
				1	2	3
4	5	6	7	8	9	10
11	12	13	14	15	16	17
18	19	20	21	22	23	24
25	26	27	28	29	30	

Do you know the date of your birthday?
How old are you?

Numbers make it easier for us to measure things.
We can use numbers to give information.
What time is it?

How fast is the car traveling?

What is the temperature?

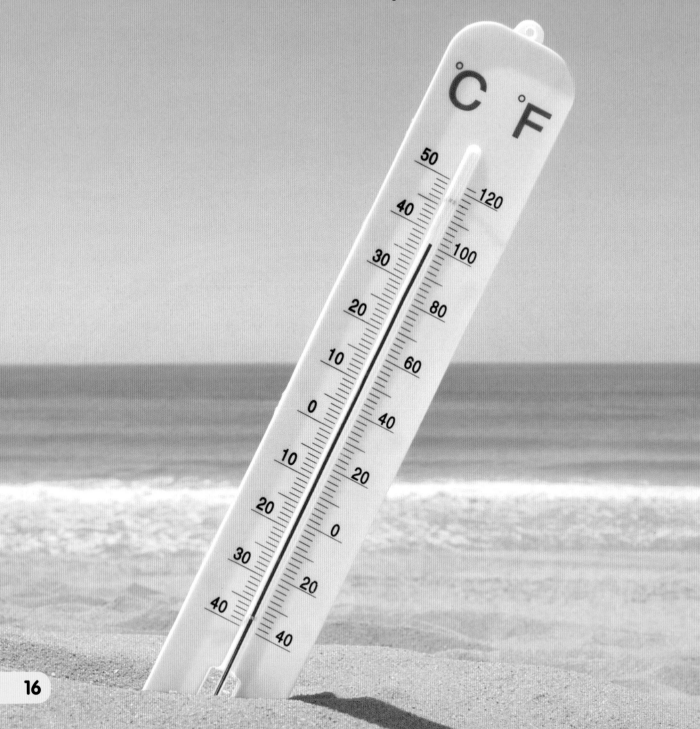

5 feet

How tall is this girl?

4 ft 6 in

4 feet

17

We use numbers when we measure height

LOW 4.1 m 13'-6" BRIDGE

and when we measure length.

We use numbers when we measure weight

and when we measure liquids.

Purchase $ 5.27

Gallons   1.938

Price Per Gallon $

Diesel ----
Regular ----
Special 2.719
Super + ----

We use numbers in sports so that each person is easy to identify.

Which car is leading in this race?

Each player has a different number on his shirt. The spectators buy programs when they go to the game. The program tells them the names and numbers of the players.

The scoreboard uses numbers to show which team is winning.

Numbers are also used to show positions—first, second, and third.

The scoreboard gives the order in which the athletes finished the race. What do the other numbers show?

	100 M INVIT.RACE MEN		WR	9.84
	FINAL		ER	9.87
1	112 GREEN M.	USA	9.79NWR	
2	101 BOLTON A	TRI	9.86	
3	103 SURIN B	CAN	9.97	
4	102 FREDERICS FR	NAM	10.02	
5	255 MITCHERLL D	USA	10.04	
6	255 MONTGOMERY T	USA	10.08	
7	215 ALFXOPOULOS A	GRE	10.22	
8	105 EZINWA OS	NGR	10.27	

What do the numbers in these pictures tell us?

3 FT

SPEED LIMIT 60

Las Vegas 72
Salt Lake City 493

SIZE 8
SHELL: 100% SILK
LINING:
100% ACETATE

DRY CLEAN ONLY

For
2 miles

1
2
3
4
5

WAY
FASHION
7 AV

OP

30 ST

25
M.P.H.

29

How many numbers can you see here? What do they mean?

30

Can you imagine what the world would be like without numbers?

Index

Reader's Guide

Visit this Scholastic Web site to download the Reader's Guide for this series:
www.factsfornow.scholastic.com Enter the keywords **Math Counts**

Library of Congress Cataloging-in-Publication Data
Names: Pluckrose, Henry, 1931– author. | Choos, Ramona G.
Title: Numbers/by Henry Pluckrose; mathematics consultant, Ramona G. Choos, Professor of Mathematics.
Other titles: Math counts.
Description: Updated edition. | New York, NY: Children's Press, an imprint of Scholastic Inc., 2019. | Series: Math counts | Includes index.
Identifiers: LCCN 2017061284| ISBN 9780531175095 (library binding) | ISBN 9780531135181 (pbk.)
Subjects: LCSH: Numbers, Natural—Juvenile literature. | Counting—Juvenile literature.
Classification: LCC QA141.3 .P58 2019 | DDC 513.2—dc23
LC record available at https://lccn.loc.gov/2017061284

Copyright © The Watts Publishing Group, 2018
Printed in Heshan, China 62

Scholastic Inc., 557 Broadway, New York, NY 10012.

1 2 3 4 5 6 7 8 9 10 R 28 27 26 25 24 23 22 21 20 19

Photos ©: cover: Neustockimages/iStockphoto; 1: Neustockimages/iStockphoto; 3: Neustockimages/iStockphoto; 4: georgeclerk/iStockphoto; 5: Coast-to-Coast/iStockphoto; 6: Kennedy Photography/Alamy Images; 7: Jirus Malawong/Shutterstock; 8: trekandshoot/Shutterstock; 9: Jeff Gilbert/Alamy Images; 10: Bianca Alexis Photography; 11: John Lund/Getty Images; 12: sumire8/Shutterstock; 13: Rawpixel/iStockphoto; 13: Zerbor/Shutterstock; 14: Stuart Pearce/age fotostock; 15: Alphotographic/iStockphoto; 16: Sergio Stakhnyk/Shutterstock; 17: Blend Images - JGI/Jamie Grill/Getty Images; 18: Jevanto Productions/Shutterstock; 19: Mike Hewitt/Getty Images; 20: Leon Neal/Getty Images; 21: George Dukin/Shutterstock; 22: simonkr/iStockphoto; 23: Lawrence Weslowski Jr/Dreamstime; 24: Natursports/Shutterstock; 25: Christian Petersen/Getty Images; 26: Superstudio/Getty Images; 27: Giuliano Bevilacqua/Getty Images; 28 top left: Michael C. Kwiecinski/Getty Images; 28 top right: WorldPictures/Shutterstock; 28 bottom left: Darren J. Bradley/Shutterstock; 28 bottom right: Tarzhanova/Shutterstock; 29 top left: Geography Photos/Getty Images; 29 top right: Julian Finney/Getty Images; 29 bottom left: magnez2/iStockphoto; 29 bottom right: Albert Pego/Shutterstock; 30: Andrey Bayda/Shutterstock; 31 background: Batechenkofff/Shutterstock; 31 girl: Masterfile/iStockphoto; 31 mailbox: goir/Shutterstock.